The Cycles

It's time to end the cycle and heal.
I wrote this book with the intention of
helping you find the light at the end of the
tunnel.
I want you to be able to feel understood
and loved because you deserve to feel all
of these things and more.
You never deserved to go through what you
went through but somehow you got yourself
in a relationship you thought had your best
interest.
This is bound to happen to anyone and I
just want to let you know that everything is
going to be alright.
May this book be a reminder that you're not
alone with your thoughts and emotions.
You're a beautiful soul inside and out who
deserves nothing but the absolute world.

# Contents


Paradise in the Sky………………………11

It's Okay to Cry………………………12

The One's………………………13

Old Poem………………………17

I'am………………………18

Forgiveness………………………19

Unloved………………………21

Nothing is the Same………………22

Switch Up………………………23

I Don't Need It, But Then I Do…………24

Possibilities………………………25

Trust Issues………………………26

Life's Way………………………27

Welcome the Pain………………………28

The Gift of the Broken………………29

Cherished Memories………………33

New World………………………36

True Beauty………………………37

Always Winning………………………38

Moving On………………………39

Only One Way………………………41

Wake Up………………………44

LIFE...........................................45
Re-read.......................................47
Beyond........................................48
Seeing the Good in the Bad...................49
Me, Myself, and I............................52
Priceless....................................54
The Recovery.................................56
A Soul's Mission.............................58
Be Careful...................................60
Love Lessons.................................61
A Magnificent Being..........................63
Wounds Heal..................................66
Self Destruct................................67
The End......................................68
Impossible...................................69
Anxiety......................................70
Dear Soulmate................................73
Love Life....................................75
Here or Not..................................76
Double Life..................................77
Fearless.....................................78
Wrong Crowd..................................79
Forever a Mystery............................80
Take Your Time...............................81
You're Special...............................82
Please Take Notice...........................83
Joy in the Rain..............................84

Define.................................85

Reminder...............................89

Your Gift..............................91

ASAP...................................92

Never a Loser..........................93

Relax..................................94

False Love.............................95

Reality................................96

Spring in Saturn.......................97

Higher Heights.........................98

A Game of Lust........................102

S.O.S.................................103

Spectator.............................104

Our Life Mission Rule.................105

II.XXIII.XX...........................106

The Uncertainty.......................108

Lies..................................110

Mind Wanderer.........................111

Suicide...............................115

Not Mutual............................117

You Matter............................118

Control...............................120

Magnet of Light.......................121

Broken Destinations...................123

Damaged Inner Child...................124

My Greatest Lost......................128

Diamonds..............................129

Narcissists.................................134
Unexpected Circumstances...............135
Above All.................................136
Monsters..................................137
Desperation...............................138
II.III.XXI..................................139
A Love Story..............................141
Take Care.................................142
Sorry Not Sorry...........................143
No Tomorrow..............................144
Death Talk................................145
Higher Vibrations.........................146
I Wish I Never Met You...................147
Try Again.................................149
The Ocean of Torment.....................150
Evil Projections..........................151
Your Life, Your World.....................152
Hell's Fire...............................153
Self Inflicted Scars......................154
Human Nature..............................155
Pay Attention.............................156
Realize This..............................157
A False Perception........................158
Unexpected Storm..........................159
Doves and Ravens..........................160
Intuitively Connected.....................161
Synchronized Spirits......................162

A Little Faith.................................................163
Past Lives....................................................164
A Star's Sweetest Secret.....................165
Hollow Knocks.............................................166
Beauty in Your Pain.................................168
What You're Far From.............................170
Safe..............................................................171
An Undiscovered Garden........................173
A Chance.....................................................174
Two...............................................................175
A Sacred Place..........................................176
Numb............................................................177
Fragments..................................................178
Every Little Thing.....................................179
Under Construction.................................180
Almost.........................................................181
Gone.............................................................182
No Doubt.....................................................185
Awareness...................................................186
For a Reason.............................................187
Miracles......................................................190
Dark Waters..............................................191
What True Love Feels Like...................192
Turning Clocks.........................................195
From Here on Out....................................196
Where There is Faith..............................198
Nothing You Can Do...............................199

The Good Days...................................200
Cherry Blossoms............................201
Deadly Nightmares.........................202
Tomorrow isn't Promised...................203
I Understand You.............................204
Rainy Days......................................205
Dear Lord........................................206
Broken Dreams...............................207
How Pain Grows..............................208
Dark Days.......................................209
Too Late..........................................211
Again..............................................212
Refocus...........................................214
The Exchange.................................215
Special Things.................................216
Growing Butterflies.........................217
Adversity.........................................218
The Unknown..................................219
Ride the Waves...............................220
Subconscious Withdrawal...............221
Whispering Secrets.........................222
Temporarily.....................................223
Hell's Parade..................................224
Loving Yourself...............................225
Catalyst...........................................226
Sickening........................................227
Wishful Dreams...............................228

It Was Never Your Fault.....................229

Life's Hidden Treasures.....................231

A Broken, Blind Heart.....................232

Done.....................233

I Unconditionally Loved You.....................235

Before Anything.....................236

Glorious Wings.....................237

Smile.....................238

Life Path.....................239

The Price of Life.....................240

Who Are You?.....................242

The Act.....................243

Not Okay.....................244

A Heavenly Place.....................245

The Lesson They Teach.....................246

Their Mask.....................247

Healthy Love Ties.....................248

Irony at its Finest.....................248

The Power.....................250

The Betrayal.....................251

In Your Eyes.....................252

Prove Them Wrong.....................253

Traumatized.....................254

How Scars Are Made.....................255

Pull Back.....................256

I Wish You the Best.....................257

Keep Your Head Up.....................258

Never Amount.............................259
The Cycle................................260
Turbulences.............................261
Infinite Light...........................262
The Beginning and the End.................264
The Moment..............................267
Superficial World.......................268
Guard Your Heart........................271
Changes.................................272
The Renewal.............................273
The Missing Piece.......................274
Love Will Find You......................276

"Paradise in the Sky"

When he spoke to me, he spoke in the form

of light and as my eyes watched, he shined

upon my soul bringing me the source of life.

As I stood there, I closed my eyes and I felt

a sudden warmth inside my heart.

In that moment right there and then, I knew

that in this world I'd find my peace when my

eyes would wander onto the skies.

Thank you Lord.

"It's Okay to Cry"

A tear a day keeps the pain away...

"The One's"

It is the things we chase that cause much
disturbance.
It is the fault of all this destruction.
Given the source of oxygen we cut it.
Given the ability to give life we become
murderers.
Given the soil to grow our crops we
become selfish that we cause starvation.
Given the opportunity to protect a life we
become criminals in this nation.
Given the chance of life we become
suicidal because others aren't kind so some
wish to die but are afraid of what's in the
other side.
Wanting to be righteous through religion but
we are still sinners.
Even given the will to choose we decide to
be evil.

Given the power to change things but we
let one man stand higher than all of us.
In a man made world we are blindly
controlled.
In denial of the truth because some are
afraid to fall.
So silence takes over the world.
While there's a war occurring of the things
that will never end.
There are eyes different than ours.
They live like programmed robots.
They are the heartless humans.
The one's unable to feel.
The one's unable to see.
The one's who won't set us free.
They are the dark side of the world.
The one called, "The Underworld".
It is the place that we are all actually in.
Can you not see?
Take a step outside and breathe.

See the pollution poisoning your own
world?
See the people losing control?
Do you see the poor?
The people asking for more?
We want more only to live.
Only to survive.
It is so unfair.
Categorized as wealthy and who's not.
Separated from our own rights.
Segregated from our pigmentation.
Killed because we look different.
What is this?
A world that feels like everything is just a
hallucination.
I can't tell the difference...
It is a world where life is taken right in front
of our eyes and everyone just walks by...
My mind catches everything and my heart
just wants to cry.

While my soul fights to survive only to stay

alive because "The One's" won't take mine.

"Old Poem"

They all spoke of the things that weren't
true.
They spoke so negatively but they had no
clue.
They spoke when we just felt like we
couldn't lose.
But they wanted to bruise our hearts till it
turned purple and blue.
They defeated us and we broke loose.
Now its just me against the world and I'm
so confused.
Because I thought we were going to fight
this together but all this turned into mental
abuse.
You no longer care about me, that's just not
fair.
How you just left me in this despair.
To fall deeper into my misery of hell.

"I'am"

The world's been a mysterious place to me.

I have feelings that none can describe to

me.

I have a soul that lives inside of me.

I am a person.

I am a human.

I am a living spirit of what has created me.

I am a fragment, a piece needed in order

for life's purpose to flow naturally.

I am different, there is none like me.

I am part of the Holy Spirit with God next to

me.

I am needed.

I am someone.

I'm important.

So are you.

"Forgiveness"

I've been told that forgiveness is the power
to all of the world.
That if I learn to forgive each and every one
of the ones that caused pain, I will learn
something that others won't.
The Lord knows its tough enough for the
humans we all are.
We're too prideful and believe weakness is
being brought out of us.
I honestly wonder...
To forgive the ones that hurt me...
Would they even care?
Would they laugh at me?
That, I realize I shouldn't care.
What matters is the feeling I will feel inside
of me because pain is only something that I
have created.

That I can forgive in order to relive, to

re-birth the person I was truly meant to be.

To forgive and feel free from my own

imprisonment.

"Unloved"

I may not be what you intended me to be.

But I gave you all of me.

Wasn't that enough?

"Nothing is the Same"

Everything's different.

The moon is no longer our company but a

reminder of what has changed.

The sun is the one who awakens us to our

lonely embrace.

The people are the ones who say none of

us were ever in this to stay.

Who were they to judge really?

We were never perfect in this but what can

I say...

Time keeps on going but nothing is the

same.

We're gone.

It all came to an end.

"Switch Up"

When somebody you used to hang out with
doesn't want to hang out with you anymore,
it's because the person you used to once
know is no longer there.

"I Don't Need It, But Then I Do"

Its been a while...

I guess my heart got lost.

At times I lose touch with reality and I forget

all about myself.

I give up on love.

In trying to understand its meaning in this

world.

Maybe all it simply is just a feeling.

A feeling of being needed, wanted, and

cared for.

Maybe it's all made up in our heads.

Damn...

You hear me?

Love sure is crazy.

"Possibilities"

It's possible for anything.
You just have to want it badly.

"Trust Issues"

I trusted you so much that I'll never trust someone else again.

"Life's Way"

Don't expect anything out of life.

Do not allow it to catch you by surprise.

Expect the unexpected and accept it.

Without asking questions.

"Welcome the Pain"

If you never cry you will never know what happiness is like, and if you never know what happiness is like, you'll never feel alive.

"The Gift of the Broken"

Lately I've been viewing my past as if it were a movie being played and I'm just there taking notes.
I've noticed many things.
Most of all I realized that every false person I came across with had a piece that I very much needed.
I believe those we consider mistakes are people who hold a piece that completes our soulmate.
How?
Well, you see every individual that has ever done you wrong has only taught you a lesson.
One so painful you'll never forget and hopefully never repeat.
By them doing this, they have also given you a gift.

An experience that allows you to see how

you would want that special person for you

to be.

Your soulmate was made just for you but

how would you two cross paths without

knowing the true understanding of

heartbreaks?

You know, this emotional pain must be

understood to its deepest level.

Now, the individual that has taken you there

has given you a different set of eyes to view

the world and even yourself.

Their lessons contain pieces to complete

your other half.

So this "pain" you intensefully feel was

meant to happen.

It must happen.

There is no changing destiny.

But you know what?

Because of everything you went through
you learn how you want your soulmate to
be.
You want them to be nothing like your past
relationships.
You desire someone better.
Someone who's actually there, present in
any moment.
Listening, caring, but most importantly
loving you unconditionally.
After all, you deserve this.
Life will make you suffer but it will also
make you smile.
It will take away those you love but it will
also give you someone to love.
Your pain will be rewarded.
Nothing in life happens just because.
If you don't have all the pieces it doesn't
mean it'll never be completed.

It just means you have more lessons to
learn.
This is all part of your soul's mission.
None of us are on the same path in life but
we all have someone meant for us.
Now cherish the pieces you do have now,
because on the other side your soulmate is
holding their pieces of you.
Trust in this, you're worthy of love.
Just like you're waiting, they're waiting too.
For the day you'll both say, "Till death do us
part".

"Cherished Memories"

Life will always be a reminder of time.

While you sit around reminiscing about

what could've been, time is saying it

would've never been.

There is not enough time to think of, "what

if".

This is just a waste.

A waste of your time.

A waste of your life.

Nobody is going to stick around long

enough to remind you of this.

Not enough people care.

Your needs are the least of their concern.

You only have you.

Only you can make yourself get up when

you fall.

Only you can decide, "if" you want to get

up.

It is up to us to decide on failure.

Time will only continue.

The saddest part is that it isn't going to wait

for you.

It never will.

You're only getting older, soon enough

you'll one day be wishing you were

younger.

Desiring to get back all the time you let slip

out of your hands.

Something that was in your total control is

now gone.

All for what?

False love?

Fake friends?

Regrets?

Mistakes?

With all honesty time is the only thing that

will remind you to let go of all your troubles

because if you don't, happiness will never

be achieved.

Life is time.

Time is life.

It's up to you to decide what's worth holding

on to because in the end of your time, you'll

take nothing.

But while you lay face to face with death,

take something in your soul worth

remembering so that it may live on forever

with you.

"New World"

I get lost in your eyes but I rather feel lost
than to look into the eyes of a soul that
doesn't make me feel this way.
A feeling of being in a world new to me
means more than anything and in there, I'd
rather not be found if it means being with
you.

"True Beauty"

If only you knew that the soul is worth more
than the body.
There is paradise among a heart that is
pure.
I've come across people with awing
appearances but with a soul so toxic.
What's the point of being beautiful from the
outside when on the inside you're just plain
ugly and cold?
Beautiful is the soul that knows the fruit of
the spirit.
They are like pieces of heaven on earth.
The one's capable of healing the damage
others have done.
With them hell will never exist.
Now, that is definitely a blessing to always
be grateful for.

"Always Winning"

Although we may give one hundred of
ourselves to people that give us nothing
back, there is always something awarded
to us at the end of our suffering.
As you give they will take, but as they take
you'll still win because in the end, broken
hearts still win.

"Moving On"

There's always this false aura in people
and the harsh truth is that those you loved
broke you and you will never be more than
nothing but a memory to them.
As you slowly let that sink in your mind, let
it reach into your heart as well.
Let it break you apart so you can rebuild a
stronger version of yourself.
Let the pain be felt so you can be able to let
go and move on.
Allow yourself to feel the intensity of every
emotion you've tried to run away from and
welcome it.
Accept them.
For every storm has its rainbow.
Every dark day has its sunshine.
Everyday isn't forever and pain will never
be forever.

It is only temporary, keep your head up and

always remember...

That life goes on and you must also go

along with it.

May your pain heal and may it open up

doors full of grace, glory and joy.

God bless you all.

"Only One Way"

Love has always been a game to some.
Some would go as far as to pretend as if
they're single while someone's waiting for
them at home.
Others, would start a relationship with you
just for fun, because sex is all they want.
Most struggle with commitment problems
so they'll hold on to you, saying they love
you and you're all they want...
but really are you ALL they want?
If it was, commitment wouldn't be a
problem from the start.
Many would break off a long term
relationship on purpose just to have sex
with someone else.
To then realize they made a mistake..
Is it though?

When you love, but I mean love
unconditionally, deeply, and passionately
there's no desire nor temptation for
someone new.
Your world would only revolve around your
significant other because they are all you
want, see, and need.
There's no room left in the heart for
someone else.
There is also no such thing as loving two
people.
Love is one.
It's a bond between two living souls that
can go as infinite as loving one another in
this lifetime and onto the next.
A love so true that may have reincarnated
from the past and would even last after
death in the afterlife.
Love is that powerful.

Majority are blinded, naïve, and ignorant to
the true significance of love.

Love is the possible in impossible.

Love is the miracle cure of pain.

Love rejuvenates the soul to move on.

Because...

Love is all.

In a world like this, love is the only way.

There is no longer a need for survival.

There is only, "I couldn't imagine my days
without you. If so, my life wouldn't be the
same."

For love is the only medicine that keeps us
all sane.

"Wake Up"

Finding love through sex is not love, it's just sex.

## "LIFE"

I always loved the wrong people because I
don't know what it is to love the right ones.
The "right ones" end up being exactly like
the rest and I'm not looking to be corrected
on that.
Based on personal experience I've learned
the deeper meaning of life, separating my
mind from the materialistic world.
I've learned to see the true value of this
universe.
There is an entire life all around you, all this
beauty but the world is full of ignorance and
disturbance.
If you look around, many beings would
always crave more.
Even blessed lives desire more, creating
only more stress.

In desiring more than what is unnecessary
we create dissatisfaction and unhappiness.
When we accept what we have for the
moment there is this abundance of
gratefulness.
A reminder that life is the greatest gift of
them all.

"Re-Read"

A person that doesn't see their self worth is
only creating an invitation for pain.

"Beyond"

The silence between two people speaks
more than words ever could.

"Seeing the Good in the Bad"

Why is it that we give our all to someone
who is giving us less than what we
deserve?
They are the mirror we are afraid to look
back at because we fear we won't
recognize the person staring back at us.
Those we decide to share the innermost
parts of ourselves are only revealing bits
and pieces of the shadows we ignore
within.
Who we really are reflects on our significant
other.
They can either show us pure light or
darkness for they are only mere reflections
of our own selves.
When we accept to be disrespected by
someone we believed loved us, we are
lacking self love.

We tend to forget the meaning of self worth
and what it truly means to love and be
loved.
Although this points at nothing else but a
red flag, there is always enough time to
save ourselves.
You shouldn't allow anyone to make you
feel like you don't deserve the world nor like
if you're not enough.
You're actually MORE than enough, but
because you're hurt you've become blinded
by those who've stolen your smile and
value to this world.
Know that you are PRICELESS.
Know that you are PRECIOUS.
Know that you are BEAUTIFUL.
You are all of these things and even
MORE.

Someone who isn't giving you attention is
only reminding you that you are not a
priority in their life.
Do not see this and feel hurt, see this as a
way of having all the reasons for letting go.
For this person is only showing you what
you mean to them through their actions.
Listen to the silence of their absence and
let time do the talking.
Take this time to focus on yourself by doing
the things you love or by simply doing the
things you've always wanted to do.
Try something new even if it means facing
your fears.
You'll discover parts of you, you thought
never existed because sometimes you
have to lose in order to win.

"Me, Myself, and I"

Maybe its true.

I've heard people say that I don't know how

to love so that's why I'm alone.

I've heard them say I'm ungrateful, that I

don't deserve the world.

I've been told I'll never have a friend

because I'm too cold.

They've said that love will never be for me.

That's why nobody is there for me.

Maybe it's true.

They said I'm a rude non-caring person

who will soon pay the price.

That Karma will go after me.

A punishment I must face to learn one of

the lessons of life.

Maybe all of it is true but let me tell you the

truth.

I've never been loved quite right.

I've been left alone with my tears
sometimes.
I've been called weak for loving too hard.
I've been naïve, bullied by the people
closest to me.
I've been hurt.
Betrayed.
Abandoned.
Unforgiven.
Laughed at from all my confessions.
It's true though.
I'm meant to be alone because those who
had my heart never understood me.
It's because they never had me.
I always had myself.
I am all I have.

"Priceless"

Love me while I am yet still nothing.

For I do not hold a pot of gold yet.

Do you not see I am still someone not

made of steel but of love and dreams?

I may not hold all the answers you seek but

I can make you feel a feeling you might

have never felt.

It is worth more than the money you wish to

grow on trees.

For there is nothing as valuable as me.

I come as one, incomplete yet willing to be

a part of you until we fully complete.

Hold me for every moment given because I

do not last long, my time is limited.

Have you looked into my eyes?

Did you see what others can't see?

Can you tell me what it is you feel for me?

As you sleep do you dream of me?

When you hold my hand do you feel safe
with me?
Do you ask yourself these questions when
you think of me?
I yet yearn for a touch so loving one strong
enough that helps me forget about the
darkness.
I want to hear you speak of love like you've
been desperate your whole life just to find
it.
Love me like you've never loved someone
else, make that your promise.
For I am more than nothing.
I am priceless.

"The Recovery"

How come we're after those who don't want
us?
A desperate attempt to make them fall in
love with us when we know that's
impossible.
We force destiny to make choices that
weren't meant for us.
We find lust instead of love.
From that we form hatred and resentment
towards an emotion we ourselves created.
We fight with time, praying for a faster way
to recover but were as numb as ever.
Yesterday still feels like today.
Tomorrow feels like never.
The days feel like forever.
There's no difference.
There's no desire in finding someone else.

We don't miss the past nor do we look
forward to the future.
Stuck in the present, it's almost as if time
isn't moving.
We're desperate.
Desperate to feel better.
Desperate to escape the inevitable.
So, we accept that it was all a lesson
destined for us.
No matter what we do, we can't escape our
fate.
There might be no control over what life
does to us, but we have control over our
emotions and these are the ones that
deserve a prayer.
There's healing for those who believe in the
higher one.
There's a life waiting to be lived by us but
first we have to wake up.
Recovery is on the way, just don't give up.

"A Soul's Mission"

There is such a thing, a belief I have that
broken souls do exist.
It is an emotion so destructive.
A being suffering from apathy.
A body existing but yet feeling dead inside.
It is a mind full of dreams that die slowly as
time passes by.
It is a heart who's been hurt thousands and
thousands of times.
A cry for help to escape our existence.
A soul so lost it's forgotten it's even a
person.
There's no longer any purpose.
It feels as if impossible to move forward.
But somehow we're still needed by the
world.

It's insane to be broken but our existence is
a reminder that we still have a purposeful
mission to accomplish.

"Be Careful"

Anyone can fuck you but not everyone can
love you.

"Love Lessons"

Its crazy how things happen.

Like you're literally gone.

But, I've learned not to fight with the things

that weren't meant for me.

I learned to stop loving you when you're not

next to me.

I learned to let go of the ones that don't

love me.

I learned to live free when everything feels

out of place for me.

I learned so much honestly...

That you never really loved me.


- Maybe the only way to find true love is by

failing in love like getting hurt and

heartbroken. That way we'll know what we

want out of a relationship. We'll go through

all the phases of love this world has, but I know that in the long run we'll find something real. Something special and simply just meant for us.

"A Magnificent Being"

It ended but its a new beginning.

Another chapter in my life.

The things I once held in my hands are no

longer there.

The love I once felt is now gone from my

heart.

The friends I once had are no longer in my

life.

The knowledge I do have now I thank God.

That his faith is the only thing that taught

me to let go.

To know that what is mine will be mine and

what isn't must go back.

If it goes, it leaves for a reason.

If it returns then its mine for all the lovely

seasons.

Cause all the heavenly things are holy.

So divine that there's no returning.

There's no space for worries.

No tears at any given moment, just infinite glory.

A pedestal high enough for the whole world to see the bond that God has given.

A blessing for all the living to see that love exists through him and through him we will be pleased.

We will all pray for one day to be living that same dream.

No other spirit but his can teach us the meaning of love2.

Through the seas and all the earthly things will need to believe.

Believe in his almighty power.

Creator of all living.

A magnificent being.

Love flows but the world doesn't know.

That some humans are false souls.

They do not know how to nurture the love

that has been handed by the savior of this

world.

They do not appreciate.

They are nothing but ignorant.

Cruel and only taking the world's

innocence.

That love is vanishing.

So, pray for love to find its way into your

heart once again because the Lord knows

all your pain.

"Wounds Heal"

Eventually love will find its way into your

heart and you'll once again be born to live

as if yesterday didn't hurt.

"Self Destruct"

But still, we love those who don't deserve

us.

"The End"

So many chances given, you walked out

my life as if you had many.

"Impossible"

I can't show you something you don't want

to feel.

"Anxiety"

The walls are slowly closing in, my mind is
losing, my heart has been fooled with.
I can't count the times I've encountered this
place.
It's the loneliness creeping up on me
creating room for unwanted thoughts.
I'm here rewinding my memories like a
movie screen.
They're rapidly playing, shifting my
emotions drastically.
I can't prevent this, as much as I wish I
could, I can't change my destiny.
It's moments like this where desiring death
is the reason we have to stay alive.
To defeat our demons that flame up the fire
in our lives.
Disastrous ending, flooding faces.

Teary moments we held tight onto our
blankets.
Griping on life because they say there's a
reason we're all here.
So we just have to try...
They say love is the cure, but it's a cure so
deadly it might reverse itself into poison if
you love the wrong person.
Friends and family blend with the mist like
ghosts.
They say family is everything but where are
they when you're all alone?
Face to face with your demons, they have
forgotten that you're only a prayer away.
Did they care enough to make a call?
Not to talk about themselves but to ask
about your life and your health.
A physical appearance can be misleading.
When the chaos is occurring in the mind
the abuse is blindly being denied.

"I'm ok, I'm fine"

But really you're screaming for help but

you're embarrassed because they say

that's a weak sign.

So, you silence the world while your mind is

at war.

You cry behind closed doors.

You fight it all just to find happiness and

feel whole again but reality is you lost

yourself a while back when you gave your

love to those who couldn't love you back.

So you've hidden yourself.

You no longer love yourself, nor do you

love at all.

You become numb because the world

became numb towards you.

For all of those reasons, you've let go.

"Dear Soulmate"

A part of me believes in a real man.
The definition of his strength and loyalty.
The way he values a woman is still
unknown to me,
but I guess that comes with age.
Maybe I believe in such a thing because I
was created from man.
We are one and I know this from the depth
of my soul.
I know that he's out there waiting to find me
and I know someday we will cross paths in
the most unexpected way life would let us
know.
For now we are becoming who we need to
be for each other.
We're going through the struggles of heart
breaks and holding on to this belief that
true love still exists.

We're keeping it alive.

For I know I didn't come into this world to
be alone.

It's a mystery to feel so empty but still know
that you're out there somewhere waiting for
me.

It might be years from now who knows but
whenever we cross paths just like God
planned, I want you to know that I'll love
you to the very end of me.

You are the one and after you there is no
one.

- Because of my belief in you, I know I am
more than enough.

"Love Life"

In an attempt to finding happiness
I found insanity.

"Here or Not"

The abyss of the unknown is the reason I
still feel alone.

"Double Life"

Many men will cheat on the women they
never intend to leave.

"Fearless"

They say that if you love too hard you might
never find yourself again.
Then what's the point of falling in love if
we're too scared to love to begin with?
I say, go ahead and lose yourself.
For there is no greater feeling than to love
and be loved.

"Wrong Crowd"

Always remember that as long as you keep hanging around the wrong people, you'll always feel out of place.

"Forever a Mystery"

Do not try to figure out life, for out of all the things in the world it is by far impossible.

"Take Your Time"

People say don't search for love.

Its true, you can't find something in

someone without completely knowing them.

You can't build a foundation with them if

they don't love you.

Love is to be felt within the heart.

For love is sacred, build it with someone

worthy of your time and presence.

"You're Special"

I hope that you realize that within you lives
everything you've been looking for

"Please Take Notice"

The reason they keep hurting you is
because they never gave a fuck about your
happiness.

"Joy in the Rain"

These moments where everyone pushes

me to the side are the moments I become

strong.

You see, pain at times allows you to see

the beautiful things in life.

"Define"

All my life I've let others define me.
They always made me feel like I was the
odd one.
I felt so different compared to many and
honestly this is a negative emotion because
you feel like you don't fit in anywhere.
By feeling like you don't belong, you create
this place in your mind where you're
constantly judging yourself and even
changing things about yourself to, "fit in".
The question here is, "why?"
Why put yourself in a position of depression
when the problem here is, you just been
misunderstood by the people around you
all your life.
There actually isn't anything wrong with
you.
You're not weird, you're just unique.

You're not odd, you're just YOU.

Being you is the most beautiful thing in the world because there will forever only be ONE version of you.

No one, and I mean NO ONE can be YOU, so take pride in that!

Stop surrounding yourself with people who will never understand you.

Each person has a mind of their own, so, see each mind as a world.

Some world's aren't meant for us, this is where we must exit and find like-minded people we can make real life connections with.

These are the people that will understand your soul.

These are the people that will respect who you really are.

These are the people who will be grateful to have crossed paths with you.

Even if you're going through a rough time in your life that you find yourself alone, don't be afraid.

This is the Universe's way of showing you how to find your higher self.

Through this time NEVER let anyone define who you are.

The only person who can ever define you is YOU.

You must realize that you are powerful and you are the one in control of your life, don't just welcome people in your life.

Know that your time is precious and you are valuable, so pick those who deserve to see the wonderful person you are in and out.

As long as YOU know who you are in this world, nothing else should matter.

You're the creator of your reality.

YOU CREATE YOUR HAPPINESS.

YOU CREATE YOUR WORLD.

YOU CREATE WHO YOU ARE.

"Reminder"

I'm here to remind you that you don't need
to waste your time on someone that doesn't
satisfy your needs.
Don't be with someone that makes you feel
like you're asking for too much when reality
is, you're not.
They just don't have that much interest in
you to care enough about your happiness.
I've realized the hard way that a man's
words don't mean anything.
What matters is their ACTIONS.
Detach your emotions from your mind and
stop fantasizing about, "what if" with
someone who ACTS like you're important.
Instead, pay close attention to their
ACTIONS and let that be the voice that
guides you to the reality you deny.

In my life I've encountered many individuals that will pretend to love you only to steal the best parts of you because they lack respect in themselves.

They take advantage of all the love YOU give because they KNOW that what you're giving them is something REAL.

Truth is they don't want you, but they also can't imagine someone else having you because you're that GOOD OF A PERSON.

This is a selfish tactic, so they hold on to you until YOU let go.

The problem is by the time you decide you deserve better you've damaged nobody else but yourself.

This is where you must dedicate time to heal your heart and learn to GIVE YOURSELF THE LOVE YOU TRULY DESERVE.

"Your Gift"

Share your knowledge only with those
whose life you know you will inspire.

"ASAP"

A man that is giving you a hard time is a man that needs to be removed out of your life.

"Never a Loser"

You will lose a couple of fake one's before

finding a real one.

"Relax"

One of our greatest mistakes in life is that
we're sometimes too hard on ourselves.
One must take it one day at a time.

"False Love"

You can never lose what was never yours.

"Reality"

While you're reminiscing about your ex,

they're busy fucking someone else.

"Spring in Saturn"

I now see why the rainbow catches feelings

for a dark sky sometimes.

The fact that you're willing to make my

gloomy days feel like sunny days, amazes

me.

I now see why the flowers need sunlight,

because without it they wouldn't bloom for a

long time.

It helps awaken the inner beauty of it and

you seem to do that just right.

When I shouldn't think of you, I do.

You make my winter feel like June.

You make my whole world in tune and if It

ever turns blue, I know that I could always

count on you.

"Higher Heights"

There's moments in my life where I am left
without words.
I stare at these blank pieces of paper and
wonder if my words are worthy to some.
I started wondering, where did I go wrong
to start having these thoughts?
It was my mistake, sometimes life switches
up and we're suddenly back to the start
where it's all dark.
That's when it becomes difficult to "see"
ourselves for who we really are.
Our own judgment pauses our goals.
It pauses our joy.
Our beliefs.
Our strength to persist.
WE are that powerful.

The strength that lives within us can be lost, where it can reverse itself into our own weaknesses.

Yet, our weaknesses can rebuild itself and once again turn into strength.

Meaning that even the strong ones fall.

Still, I'm here to remind you that you are all you got.

Our weakest moments are the strongest.

A test of where your strength and faith lies.

A reminder that if you won't chase after your dreams nobody will chase them for you, nobody will believe in them as MUCH AS YOU DO.

You might have people around you but in reality, you're on this journey ALONE.

Alone in the sense where you're the one in charge of your choices and especially your FUTURE.

Along this journey there will be supporters

helping you reach the highest vibration you

came in this life to be.

But you're THE ONE IN CONTROL.

To decide whether you want to reach the

higher heights of YOUR life.

While you're making your way to the top

you will suffer and there will be struggles.

There will be storms and there will be

chaos.

But your plan here is to NEVER STOP.

KEEP GOING.

KEEP PUSHING.

DON'T LIMIT YOURSELF, INSTEAD BE

LIMITLESS.

EXPAND YOUR MIND AND

KNOWLEDGE.

BECOME WISE AND HUMBLE

YOURSELF.

COUNT ALL YOUR BLESSINGS.

THIS JOURNEY IS YOURS AND YOURS
ONLY.
REACH THE TOP.
I'LL MEET YOU THERE.

"A Game Of Lust"

You will sometimes cross paths with
someone temporarily but because they are
no longer present in your life it doesn't
mean you've done something wrong.
It just means their time to be in your life is
done.
Thank them for the message and lesson
learned and keep moving on.

"S.O.S"

Suppressants don't cover the pain

It just helps make the pain more bearable.

We're still living a lie.

STOP.

It's time to WAKE UP.

"Spectator"

People feel the need to hold on to someone

who is unworthy because they feel as

though they can't do better.

You must first change your mind and start

visualizing yourself winning.

This way you're allowed to view yourself

out of that relationship into another position

in your life.

A spotlight where victory awaits you.

"Our Life Mission Rule"

Work on all areas of your life to build a mentality that's going to lead you to your success.

"II.XXIII.XX"

People will try to make sense out of
NONSENSE because the truth will always
be hard to accept.
Nobody likes the truth, because nobody
wants to lose.
The truth is REALITY and reality HURTS.
ACCEPT life as a simple complexity
instead of escaping your thoughts.
This is a PARADOX.
It is as simple as a yes or a no from what's
right and wrong.
We are LOGICAL beings, meaning we
INTUITIVELY know the TRUTH.
The simplicity of humanity is ACCEPTING
and CONFRONTING the REALITY of our
lives and being able to MOVE FORWARD
with the struggles and complications of
what lies ahead in the unknown.

There must be NO FEAR and true
PERSEVERANCE.
There must be NO LOOKING BACK but
one must have FAITH that there is
GREATNESS waiting for us at the END.

"The Uncertainty"

It's been a while but you've taken me into a
place I haven't visited in months.
It's cold enough to make one feel numb.
It's quiet and the silence makes me never
want to speak again for the sake of my
sanity.
It's empty, my soul is all I have in here.
It's dark and light seems to be miles away.
Your depression blinded you and it got to
me.
It's like, you left me with the monster
everyone else is afraid to see.
I saw yours and I was selfless enough to
shield you from it with all I had.
I absorbed all your pain and suddenly they
became my own.
I didn't deserve to feel all of this alone.
Still...

I didn't deserve to feel any of this at all.

But I do.

You used the word "love", like if you knew

what it was.

You pretended like I was, "the one" to make

sense of something that made no sense to

you.

You wanted to give us a meaning when

deep down from the start you knew there

was none.

I played along because they say destiny

could take you far and it was true...

I just never knew it would take me far away

from you.

"Lies"

His words were like those of a drunk man.
But instead of a drunk mind speaking sober
thoughts, he spoke of lies.
The one's convincing enough to make fairy
tales come to life.

"Mind Wanderer"

It was in the midst of my own embrace I
found comfort within.
As the world turned cold against me, I was
able to heal my wounds with patience.
I learned that not all souls want to be saved
and if one dived deep enough to rescue the
lost, we too can become the lost.
There's such a thing called, "The lost and
found" but not all souls can be found as
one thinks.
In trying I found pain and failure.
This was no ordinary task where practice
makes perfect.
No.
You cannot help those that don't want to be
helped.
You cannot save those if they do not desire
to save themselves.

You cannot change people that do not wish
to change.
In doing so I ended up with the broken.
I wondered and figured that I too was
broken.
I was the broken that knew how to fix itself.
I knew how to repair those that couldn't do
it for themselves.
I was the fixer.
I attracted these souls because my soul
was a puzzle in their lives and in my life
they were mine.
In order for me to have a deeper
understanding of my life and the world
around me I needed to absorb their pain as
if they were my own.
I used to believe these were mistakes I
caused because of poor choices but we're
all destined to go through different paths.

My so-called, "poor choices" gifted me with
spiritual growth.
Externally I am still a mystery to some while
only a few have yet seen my true colors.
Although many can't see my growth,
internally I hold in so much.
People do not need to see your every move
nor do they need to know who you are
unless they've earned a place in your life.
Treat yourself as if you were already a
Queen/King.
People need to be worthy to deserve your
presence because time is precious.
Life is beautiful but at the same time it's
very short.
You can not stay in an environment of souls
that are undeserving.
The lost must learn to find their way
because they are the only ones capable of
creating a path to freedom.

To find liberation one must have at least a
bit of love towards themselves.
That's the first step to escape this place of
wonder.
Love.
Love for oneself is the beginning of a new
chapter because you will then love others
and the world around you.

"Suicide"

Before:

How can we desire death without truly
knowing what lies beyond this realm?
This world is not perfect because of
humanity but there isn't a better life ahead
once you cut yours off.
I believe you cause the universe a sort of,
"glitch".
Lowering the vibration and causing a
chaotic chain of events to those who love
you.
That is why your existence here is needed
because you are a person that could save
others but how can you do that when all
you wish for is to be gone?

After:

How can we desire death without truly

knowing what lies beyond this realm?

This world is not perfect because of

humanity but there isn't a better life ahead

once you cut yours off.

I believe you cause the universe a sort of,

"glitch".

Lowering the vibration and causing a

chaotic chain of events to those who loved

you.

That is why your existence here was

needed because you were a person that

could've saved others but how could you do

it now that you're gone?

"Not Mutual"

Remember that although we make places
in our heart for someone special the feeling
might not be reciprocated.

"You Matter"

Just know that every good person will
always be missed because a kind heart is
never forgotten.
That's one of the main reasons they'll
always come back, but it doesn't always
mean you should allow them back in your
life.
They know that what you gave them was
real and it hurts to accept that the type of
love you made them feel will never be
found in someone else.
Through time they'll struggle to understand
the layers that there is to coming across the
love you presented them with.
Their soul still needs growth and
experience but when they've reached these
levels of the spirit you'll be remembered.

Nobody lives a peaceful life from making
another human being cry.
"You reap what you sow".

"Control"

Love isn't blind.

It's a choice where we choose to love

blindly.

"Magnet of Light"

Remember that you can't desire something
you're unable to attract.
If you aren't spiritually inclined to pursue all
your goals in life then this thing you want
won't make its way to you.
When you don't meet your expectations
you're creating unhappiness within yourself
which then lowers your vibration.
People are energies in life form and we're
the magnet.
In order to attract others we must first,
"create" a new flow of energy which then
raises the vibration in our aura.
Become the spotlight everyone wants to be
a part of.
When you are full of light others that come
in contact with your spirit will feel this vibe
and they'll become light as well.

Once you accomplish many life lessons this
concept of wanting someone or anything in
general will fade away because we've
changed our mindset.
We rewired our minds which then attracts
all the things we really deserve to have in
this lifetime.
Everything has its perfect timing, don't just
look at the light and wonder forever how'd it
be if you decided to change.
No.
Be the change and step in.
Become a magnet of light.

"Broken Destinations"

As a child I chased my dreams in the stars,

but as an adult I chased paper and broken

hearts.

"Damaged Inner Child"

At the end of the day we're still just children
who've grown old with time.
Meaning that our childhood traumas have a
lot to do with how we carry ourselves as
"adults".
We can be adults who yet yearn for many
things we missed out as a child.
Nobody but you would know and
understand your deepest desires.
You questioning why others have reached
higher places in their lives before you
doesn't mean you are less of a person.
When in reality our childhood plays a big
role in this.
The family and environment we've
surrounded ourselves with were completely
out of our control but it shaped us into who
we are today.

124

We have absolutely no control whatsoever
to choose the families we end up with and
I've always seen this as a higher plan that
to the human mind
will forever be impossible to understand.
I know that in life nothing is "impossible" but
trying to figure out life itself is one of the
things the human mind is too little to
comprehend.
Our lives go deeper than what the people
around us seem to capture.
Many don't know the depth of what made
us, "us" today.
Who we are is so complex and our past as
many say we must forget is the most
important piece.
"It" is what created us.
It is a piece we can't forget but for the sake
of our mind and health there are certain

memories we must forget in order to move forward in life.

I promise you many individuals would judge your personality and how you carry yourself because they don't know anything about you.

The minds of humans are automatically programmed to judge, to question everything and wonder, "why?".

When all the answers lie in the history and timeline of their "past".

I want you to bring out your inner child and fix those issues that are hurting you everyday.

Once you come face to face with the problems you will raise your vibration, meaning your inner light.

Raising your vibration will raise your energy, there will be a change occurring within you that those around you will notice.

It will cause you to lose many people that
you thought were close to you but as we
lose we will win in other areas of our lives.
You will then start another chapter of your
journey where you search for your inner
child because it was never lost.
Give it the attention that as a child your
mind was too innocent and naïve to
understand the world around you.
Heal this part of your past and love your
inner child for it has always been a part of
you.

"My Greatest Lost"

My greatest lost wasn't you.

My greatest lost was losing myself trying to

love you, so you can love me.

"Diamonds"

Those we chase and welcome into our life
says alot about who we are.
I find myself more indulged in my thoughts
lately, questioning those I've allowed in my
life so far.
Those we can't quite put a finger on why
we pursue them or why certain individuals
who harm us in all sorts of toxic emotional
ways, are the ones we need to focus on
and ask ourselves the reason behind our
motives.
There is no growth when you just let
anyone welcome themselves into your life.
Many of these people have evil intentions,
ones that you are unaware of.
The kindness that some of us have blinds
us to the pursuit of these souls.
It's not that you're naive nor immature.

It's just that you view the world differently.

Very different.

People with good hearts become targets for

those whose hearts aren't.

It's not your fault.

The world was made with the intention for

us to handle and deal with souls like this.

This is where you must learn to choose one

by one the people who deserve to be

among your circle.

You have to treat yourself as if you are a

Queen/King.

What does this mean?

Well, not just everyone gets to be around

such royalty, one must deserve it and this is

how you should view yourself.

You're a diamond, a precious gem.

Not everyone deserves to hold such value

in their hands.

Not everyone knows how to appreciate the
beauty of its rarity.
Not everyone can own it.
Everyone doesn't deserve you.
Everyone wasn't made for you.
You can't mold yourself into someone
you're not just to please others.
Everyone won't understand you, and that's
okay.
Your unique personality will attract those
who will appreciate the sincerity and
serenity of your soul.
You choosing to change for others will only
cause more false souls to enter into your
life.
You don't need this.
What you need is to let go of people who
have no love for you.
Love isn't always about sex.
Love can be shown in many different ways.

Hold on to those who care for you in your
lowest.

Hold on to those whose shoulders you
know you can lean on when life has struck
you.

Hold on to those who are willing to lend a
helping hand when you're at your most
vulnerable.

Hold on to those who make you smile even
when your world is shattering.

Hold on to those who listen to the stories
that are eating at your heart.

Hold on to these souls so damn tight.

They are gems.

The rarest pieces of life live among some
people and if you're willing to see the
message behind this, know that you are
one of those souls who hold one within.

You're a diamond.

The symbol of light and love.

A piece of heaven right in front of their eyes

and darling, not everyone was meant to

see heaven.

"Narcissists"

People stuck in hell can't see angels.

For those reasons, they'll never be grateful

of your existence.

"Unexpected Circumstances"

Life is a surprise, so when shit happens
don't be surprised.

"Above All"

When you walk with God, you only fear

God.

No one else.

"Monsters"

Monsters can't love humans.

They're monsters.

So, why do you keep going back to them?

Is it the fact that we're loving so damn

blindly?

The fact that we lack self love.

The fact that we're dealing with issues of

low self esteem, causes many of us to fall

in love with our own demons in the dark.

"Desperation"

Loneliness invites anything and
Loneliness loves everything.

"II.III.XXI"

The HUMAN MIND will ALWAYS find every
LITTLE excuse to the things they KNOW
aren't right.
That is PART of the flesh.
To NOT listen and to PRETEND.
To IGNORE the TRUTH that it KNOWS.
Being HUMAN isn't easy but the HEART
and SPIRIT knows the truth of WHY we
came into this world and the IMPORTANCE
of each and every Soul's role.
So, to sit there and feel meaningless is a
LACK OF LOVE towards oneself.
You are HERE!
ALIVE!
Meaning YOU HAVE PURPOSE, don't you
ever let anyone tell you otherwise.
THERE IS NO OTHER ANSWER.
YOU ARE THE ANSWER.

YOU ARE THE PURPOSE.
FOLLOW YOUR HEART AND LIVE UP TO
IT!

"A Love Story"

I once saw a forever with you and now, all I see is a love story that ended way too soon.

"Take Care"

I get it.
You don't know how to keep a good thing
because life always gave you the worst of
everything and I'm sorry the people you
came across treated you so bad but I hope
in crossing paths with me you'll believe in
better things.
So...
Even though I had to walk out of your life...
I hope you find what you couldn't find in me
in someone else.
I truly, truly do.
Now, you take good care of yourself and
never forget...
You were one of the most beautiful things
my hands have ever caressed.

"Sorry not Sorry"

You should've loved me when I cared.

"No Tomorrow"

Be a little fiercer and love a little harder

because our time here is limited.

So, don't be afraid.

Show me your heart dear and watch me

love you like there's no tomorrow.

"Death Talk"

Sweet lips leave bloody stains.

Erotic touch leave crippling pain.

What have you done to me?

You've brought me back to life just to kill me

again!

"Higher Vibrations"

Everytime you take a step away from toxicity you're choosing to love yourself.

"I Wish I Never Met You"

I don't understand how you could stare

deeply in my eyes and still tell a lie...

I don't comprehend the love you so badly

feel towards me when you were still holding

on to your past.

I really don't get it and that's why I won't

continue to stick around.

I'm devastated because I'm stuck here

reminiscing while you're over there still

contemplating.

Man, I swear this is why I hate catching

feelings.

Dealing with these aching memories.

You really don't fucking get it.

How the touch of your skin has become my

deadly addiction and how your kiss had the

power to save me.

This all feels like a damn mistake and now

I'm drowning in my own regrets.

You have no idea...

How much I wish I never met someone like

you.

"Try Again"

Your eyes will always hold the truth

of all the lies

your lips try to conceal.

"The Ocean of Torment"

If you don't love, respect, and cherish

yourself, you will drown yourself in people

that never deserved you.

"Evil Projections"

I wish someone would've told you about the
beautiful, greatness in you instead of
projecting the worst and ugliest things
about themselves into you.

"Your Life, Your World"

You are not what people say you are.

You are what you believe you are.

This is your world.

Live it right and live it fairly.

Don't let anyone rob you of your identity

and self worth.

"Hell's Fire"

You tried to find the Sun in someone that
never lived in the light.

"Self Inflicted Scars"

Your flaws and faults may come back to
haunt you in the form of a person.
They will cast out your inner light just to fill
you with their darkness.
Your past mistakes will repeat itself and
you'll begin to believe the worst about
yourself, only because you weren't strong
enough to love yourself and let go of them
when you needed to.

"Human Nature"

You might've made a mistake and gotten
yourself in the turmoil you're in.
It's complicating and frustrating to explain
but know that your most challenging and
chaotic moments in life are the most life
changing one's because just like the sky
will always be in need of the rain, your soul
will always be in need of growth.
In every waking day of your life you are
meant to experience all of the daily
unexpected occurrences it may bring.
It is part of this world and the life cycle of a
human being.
Because...
You are meant to forever grow and
transform into who you're truly meant to be.

"Pay Attention"

Most of the feelings you feel about
someone aren't made up.
They're existing within you for a reason.
Whether it's good or bad, never ignore
them.

"Realize This"

I'm sorry someone made you feel like you deserve to feel everything they've put you through.
Just know, it's not your Karma nor is it Fate.
It's abuse.

"A False Perception"

Stop trying to find the person they were in
the beginning.
It was all a false image.
A ghost your mind must stop chasing.
Please, understand this.

"Unexpected Storm"

Let the rain be a reflection of all the things
no one else sees.
For many beautiful things bloom when all
seems doomed.

"Doves and Ravens"

My head spins at the thought of your
choices and my heart fumbles to accept the
reality you manifested.

"Intuitively Connected"

I'm a big believer of the unseen things.
So, what my eyes have yet not seen, my
heart has already felt.

"Synchronized Spirits"

Hearts that feel the same, will forever beat
the same.

"A Little Faith"

All the beautiful things in life will come to
you when you're ready to receive them.
When your heart, soul, and mind becomes
one with the Universe.
It is then, you'll know what peace feels like.
All you have to do is have a little faith and
believe in the things that feel impossible to
you.
That is how your dreams will come true.

"Past Lives"

I have loved you for lifetimes before this
one.

"A Star's Sweetest Secret"

Never for a second believe that love is

complicating or that you're too hard to

understand and adore.

Please, remove these thoughts out of your

mind because somewhere in this gigantic

planet you're someone's truest desire.

You're their...

**Everything.**

"Hollow Knocks"

I look at you and wonder where'd it all
went...
All the seasons just flew past us and we
never noticed it.
So much time wasted on nonsense.
All because honesty wasn't in your plans.
Somehow, I learned to play your games.
And...
That didn't help much but cause more pain.
When...
All I wanted was to find a piece of Heaven
through the touch of your hands.
Instead...
I found more broken pieces of myself.
And...
It's getting harder and harder everyday to
just pretend.
As if...

My heart still lives inside of my chest.

167

"Beauty in Your Pain"

The truth you seek lives no where else but
within you.
So...
Allow yourself to feel what deeply hurts.
Allow yourself to breathe in the very place
that tries to suffocate you.
Allow yourself to be free there instead of
always trying to escape it.
Feel the wrath of your own inner war and
surrender.
For you do more harm to yourself fighting a
fight you never deserved to find.
But...
It found you.
And...
It has taken too much of what's left of you
but remember...
It doesn't have to continue to be this way.

So, close your eyes and breathe.

It's okay.

Because...

This my dear sweet friend, is no where

near the end.

It is truthfully only the beginning of

something beautiful.

Something, not even you were expecting.

For there is beauty in your pain.

Oh, yes.

There truly is.

"What You're Far From"

There is a path meant for you to follow but
you will never be looked down on if the
challenges you face along your way
change your perspective on life.
This is bound to happen because you are
simply a human being and you carry
something within you that was created to
go through thousands, if not millions of
transformations in its lifetime.
You are not meant to be the same person
you were a few years ago because through
this journey you will get lost and you'll
constantly question the reasons behind
such occurrences, but I need you to always
keep in mind that you're far from being a
failure.

"Safe"

If you ever get the chance to love

someone...

Love them unconditionally and love them

fairly.

Love them in all the ways you'd love to be

loved and make this your most important

promise.

And...

Whenever you get this chance...

Remind them of their place in your life.

Because...

This journey isn't promised to last long but

while you're here...

Make your time with them worthwhile.

Give them the best of you and nothing less.

Give them all of you until there's nothing

left.

Give them what no one else could ever

give you.

This way...

They'll always feel safe with you.

"An Undiscovered Garden"

Even when the rain continues to fall on you,
you're still beautiful.
You believe that no one can see your pain
when it begins to pour, but those little water
droplets resemble much more than what
you portray to the world.
They are all of the things you will never
show and through them you allow yourself
to release what hurts.
You hide among the clouds, not knowing
that the sun awaits you.
It watches over you when you believe that
no one sees you.
Although, in here you feel out of place you
are in all reality the center of its attention.

"A Chance"

With time all things fall into place.
So, do not stress over anything you can't
control.
Things are the way they are for a reason.
Many don't need an explanation when your
heart knows you better than you know
yourself.
Now, this time...
Just give it a chance and listen to what it
has to say.
Because the truth is...
It's been trying to save you all along when
you failed to save yourself.

"Two"

You can try but somethings will always

break because in a relationship it takes two

to fix things...

Not one.

"A Sacred Place"

Never build your happiness around people.

Build it around yourself.

This way...

You'll never feel alone.

"Numb"

Things haven't been the same for me.

I no longer see myself the way I used to.

I'm sure this is what it feels like to lose

yourself in someone else.

Because...

Once you've given up your heart, you're no

longer whole.

Your emotions are no longer yours.

You're a walking corpse, numb from the

toxicity of what's supposed to be called...

Love.

"Fragments"

The person you look for are bits and pieces

of all the things missing in you.

But...

Remember, that without a doubt they are

fragments of all the things you can solely

be for yourself.

"Every Little Thing"

That heart of yours...
That sweet, sweet heart of yours deserves
every little thing it dreams of.

"Under Construction"

Build a home within yourself.

"Almost"

Because of you...

I almost forgot who I was.

"Gone"

It's days like today that I wonder what I've

gotten myself into because I can hardly

recognize the person I once fell in love

with.

It's like suddenly you're living with a

complete stranger and this feeling seems to

come and go but it lingers longer as the

days, weeks, and months continue to pass

by.

You continuously lie to yourself by

pretending you don't know why this feeling

is living within you and you tell yourself that

in any day, things will hopefully change.

But...

It's not your fault to think this way.

You're in love and you can't help but hope

for things to get better someday.

Yet...

It's a very dangerous place to be in when
you know the truth.
It's extremely harsh to accept and difficult
to live with because it makes you feel...
So, empty, lost and broken.
So, lonely, sad and misunderstood.
So, far from feeling like your old self, that it
all becomes overwhelming.
Almost...
Too much to handle.
You're anxious over things that are now
completely out of your control.
And...
You're desperately reaching for someone
who will never love you the way you wished
they did.
It's...
Heartbreaking having to accept that the
person whose eyes you're deeply looking
into today is...

Gone.

"No Doubt"

One thing I can say without a single doubt
in my heart is that I loved you in a way I
have never loved anyone else.

"Awareness"

Healing begins when you acknowledge
your past and become highly aware that
the change you want begins the moment
you let go.

"For a Reason"

If you sit down and look back at everything
you've ever been through you'll realize that
you've only grown.
From the first day God placed you here
your soul started its journey to grow into
who he destined you to be.
Nothing in your life will remain the same.
No matter how bad you want it to.
Things will only continue to change
because they're meant to.
You can't fight against destiny.
You can only fight against yourself.
It is the only control you truly have in this
life.
Because...
Nothing here is yours and no one here is
yours.
It is all given.

Yet...

It is temporary and what you do with it is all

up to you.

So, if you can...

Love and cherish every moment.

Build beautiful memories.

One's you can smile at when you're old and

gray.

Make the best of your time here and fill

your mind up with all kinds of magnificent

things.

Let the light, love and joy of life rule the

palace of your heart.

Forget about the irrelevant things.

You know, about...

The things that hurt badly.

Those don't serve any purpose.

Nor...

Will they ever serve their purpose.

Focus on your growth and the areas in your
life you can improve.
Learn to let go when you must and cling
onto the desires of your spirit.
Know that there are many, if not thousands
and thousands of lessons behind our pain
and suffering but the outcome of it will
always lead us back to love.
Don't let the superficiality of this world blind
you of what's true in you.
Just...
Don't become like everyone else.
Be you every blessing day you get and
never let anyone steal your light.
Because...
You came into this world for a reason.
An unimaginable, mysterious, beautiful
reason.

"Miracles"

Your heart heals a little

everyday you whisper a prayer.

"Dark Waters"

The thing is, you have to learn how to navigate through the dark waters of life.

"What True Love Feels Like"

I'm sorry someone made you feel as if
believing in love is childish.
You honestly never deserved to be put
through any of the things they've put you
through.
You don't deserve to be told things about
you that aren't true.
You don't deserve to be put down because
of things that were said and done in the
past.
You don't deserve to live everyday feeling
like a burden to them.
You just don't...
You deserve to be held and loved
wholeheartedly.
You deserve to be reminded of your worth
and you deserve to be kissed as if you

were the only person that they see in their

world.

Because...

Your dreams and desires shouldn't only

exist within you.

They should live outside of you and all

around you forever.

Why?

Because...

Your Universe shouldn't be so deserted.

It shouldn't feel so lonely and it also

shouldn't feel so unfixable.

It should feel as if everyday you're

witnessing a miracle.

Feeling an impossible but yet so possible

feeling.

One so indescribable that you'll want to

discover it over and over again in every

lifetime God blesses you with because one

lifetime just isn't enough.

So, yes.

This is what you truly deserve.

A million times;

"Yes!"

Because...

This right here darling is, what true, pure,

unconditional love feels like.

"Turning Clocks"

What hurts me the most somedays to
accept is that I can't turn back the clock.
Maybe that way you and I would've made
less mistakes.
Maybe just maybe...
We could've learned how to love each other
better instead of causing so much pain.

"From Here on Out"

Your mind is one of the most powerful
things in you.
It can cause havoc in your life if you let it
run wild because majority of the time all the
things you think don't have a solution,
actually have one.
Some are harder to accept than others but
it is necessary for the safety of your mental
health.
While other thoughts and problems need to
be set free.
Don't cage yourself up in a head space
where you feel like everything around you
is against you because things aren't
working in your favor.
See the problem and all the lessons it's
teaching you.

Observe your mind but don't believe
everything you think about yourself.
Don't even believe what others think of you.
They're not you and they will never get a
peak of that wonderful heart and soul of
yours.
So, why even bother wasting precious time
of your life thinking about people and things
that aren't even true?
So, please always believe in yourself no
matter what happens from here on out,
never give up on who you truly are.

"Where There is Faith"

Be fearless and carry your faith like a
wielding sword.
For where there is faith, there is an
abundance of infinite strength and love.

"Nothing You Can Do"

Don't feel bad for yourself.

People come and go.

But...

Always remember...

It is completely out of your control.

No matter what you do.

No matter what you say.

No matter how you feel.

There's nothing you can do.

You can't force someone to love you but

you can force yourself to let go of them and

love yourself again.

"The Good Days"

Somedays...

I find myself missing who you used to be.

"Cherry Blossoms"

Holding on to you hurts just as much as
letting you go.

"Deadly Nightmares"

The scariest thing wasn't loving you.
The scariest thing was how dead you made
me feel for loving you.

"Tomorrow isn't Promised"

I just wanted you to love me in such a
profound way because you knew I might
not be here tomorrow.

"I Understand You"

I know your mind tends to wander in
moments it shouldn't but you can't help it,
it's just the way you are.

"Rainy Days"

Allow yourself to feel what you've been
trying to run away from.
Feel it and know that it's okay.
Remember, it's only temporary.

"Dear Lord"

Know that everything you've ever searched
for will never be found.
Do not look for what you want.
Just ask our dear Lord and patiently wait
for it.

"Broken Dreams"

I know you wonder why does it hurt so
much and it's because you believed too
much in a dream, you knew you shouldn't
have dreamt of.

"How Pain Grows"

The truth has always been there.

You simply just always ignored it because

you managed to convince yourself that

things will hurt less this way.

"Dark Days"

You always made me feel like a stranger.

No matter if I was there or not.

You always made me feel like you didn't

care.

And...

The most painful part was watching you

chase after someone who never gave a

fuck about you.

All their narcissistic self cared about was

how much damage they could inflict on you

just to get a reaction out of you and it broke

me every single day to witness this.

So, I got tired of waiting around.

Tired of trying.

Tired of loving.

Tired of trying to convince you to see in me

what only I could see in myself.

Because...

You never choose me back then and I
learned to live with the fact that you never
will.

"Too Late"

The sad part out of all of this is, you'll
realize who I am in your life right after I'm
gone and by then, it'll be too late.

"Again"

I'd say it was bittersweet to have fallen in
love with you.
To witness myself go through hell and back
for you anytime and any day was
astonishing.
It was as though, there was nothing you
could ever do that was enough for me to
walk out on you.
Absolutely nothing and that's why I always
stayed.
Because...
What I felt inside for you overpowered
anything.
No matter what anyone said, the feelings
were that great.
And...
I think that's what hurts more than anything
right now.

Thinking that the more I gave you the more

you'd want to stay.

But...

I guess that wasn't the case.

Instead, you always found any reason to

run away.

Leaving me behind in a place I haven't

visited in years.

And...

I would have never imagined that you were

capable of taking me back here...

Again.

"Refocus"

The best thing you can do for yourself is
control your emotions.
Learn how to control your reaction to
somethings.
So, refocus and stay calm.

"The Exchange"

Someday you'll have to allow someone to
know you for who you really are and I
mean, REALLY know you.
Make it ONE person.
Know that this is important.

"Special Things"

Know that whatever can make you smile on
a terrible day is something that pulls on the
strings of your heart.
Please, hold on to it and cherish it always.

"Growing Butterflies"

In life you are meant to break because there's changes you're meant to go through.
This is a necessary step to reach your destination.

"Adversity"

Changes will come to us all.
You have to embrace it.
You have to accept them and
you have to face them head on.

"The Unknown"

Don't worry too much about trivial things.

Just, listen to your heart.

Let it be your guidance into the unknown.

It knows more than you know.

"Ride the Waves"

Don't be afraid of what you feel when what
you feel is there to teach you all about
yourself.

"Subconscious Withdrawal"

Too much pain forces the soul to change.

"Whispering Secrets"

There is something very beautiful inside all
of us.

"Temporarily"

Our hearts have been open for far too long,

it's time to temporarily close it off in order

for us to feel what we've been giving out.

"Hell's Parade"

I wonder, what gives a person the right to
pick a day to disrespect, misbehave and
mistreat you?

"Loving Yourself"

At the end of the day nobody knows what
you're really going through, so take care of
yourself as best as you can.

"Catalyst"

I would've never thought that you'd be the
catalyst to all the things I feel right now.

"Sickening"

It makes me sick to my stomach to believe
that what you gave me was love.

"Wishful Dreams"

I just hope someday, somehow, you find
what you're searching for.

"It Was Never Your Fault"

There's nothing wrong with you.
There's literally nothing wrong with the way
you feel and think.
You are who you are for a reason and you
feel these things deeply because you're
meant to.
So, please don't blame your beautiful heart
anymore.
Don't make yourself suffer anymore.
Don't think too much of anything that hurts
you anymore.
This just creates another bad day and you
don't deserve that.
Just loosen your grip on all the things
you're desperately trying to keep a hold of.
Because...
You're hurting yourself.

Reminiscing constantly over the past and

how things used to be.

Accept that things have changed and that

there's a possibility that it might not go back

to the way they were.

And...

That's okay.

This is life and you know that love can

either go two ways.

But...

God works for the good of those who love

him.

Everything will sort itself out.

I promise.

"Life's Hidden Treasures"

Although, there's a few things in your life
that isn't working out, know that there are
hundreds of other beautiful things to be
grateful for.

"A Broken, Blind Heart"

Acceptance isn't easy but it's necessary.

This is pure bliss to the soul.

"Done"

The thing is, you're nothing like the person
you presented yourself to be and I think
that's the problem now.
Accepting that everything we've built was
all a lie.
I hang on to these photos of us because
that's all I have left of us to remember.
But...
I know that's not who you are.
So...
I ask myself, what's the use in pretending to
live a life with you that you no longer want?
What's the use in me chasing after you
when you continuously go back to your old
ways?
I keep waiting, expecting you to change
any day now but the cycle keeps repeating

and I'm just so damn exhausted of denying

how terrible you make me feel.

And...

It shouldn't be this way.

It shouldn't feel like this...

Like...

It shouldn't hurt this bad.

It just shouldn't.

So...

I'm done.

"I Unconditionally Loved You"

I wish you knew what I felt for you the
moment my eyes spotted you.
You felt like my forever after, the one I was
willing to go through hell and back for.
There was nothing that could make me
walk out on you and I just wish that you
would've felt the same.

"Before Anything"

Don't find anyone just yet.

Find yourself first and in that same space

learn to love who you are.

"Glorious Wings"

Beauty still shines through pain.

You just have to look a little deeper.

Inspect every little detail to see clearly the

hidden message.

It's a beautiful secret for you to endeavor of

an amusing experience you'll always

remember.

Full of love and hate.

Full of laughter and tears.

Full of strength and pain.

Yet...

It all makes sense.

How you grew and grew those glorious

wings.

"Smile"

Attach your heart to all the things
that make you smile.

"Life Path"

There are many life paths to travel on but
your heart only knows about one.

"The Price of Life"

There is no need to pretend.

No need to distract yourself.

No need to keep wondering.

All you need is to allow yourself to feel all

the things you've been running away from.

Indulge yourself in everything you believe

you're not strong enough to face.

Then take a look around your

surroundings...

Nothing can compare to the life you're

given.

It's not about what you have and don't

have.

It's about the gift you've been granted.

So, when your mind begins to fill itself up

with irrelevant things...

Take a deep breath and look outside.

Absolutely nothing can compare to the
marvelous price of life.

"Who Are You?"

I hardly recognize you that I'm confused.

Who was the person you introduced me to?

Because...

He's nothing like the one I'm meeting now.

And...

That's so damn frightening.

"The Act"

You turned me into a billion shattered
pieces.
Never in my life have I felt so helpless and
it's so sad because I can't really explain it.
How you could create these cycles just for
the hell of it.
How you could use all that I was and make
of me all that I am today.
How you could create so much chaos and
act as if nothing ever happened.

"Not Okay"

It's okay to be at fault for somethings.

What's not okay, is not acknowledging the

fact that you committed them.

That's psychological abuse.

Something no one should endure.

"A Heavenly Place"

One day...

You'll get lost in a beautiful place where
you'll never want to be found.

"The Lesson They Teach"

Isn't it crazy, how all this time...

You continued to hold on, when they've

ALWAYS shown you all the reasons to let

go.

## "Their Mask"

A liar is quick to add more lies to their lies.
That's the only time they'll actually stop the
argument they purposely started and "try"
to discuss about your suspicions so you
wouldn't find out about the things they're
hiding.
How ironic is it though, that in that moment
they want to seem and sound genuine and
honest when the truth is, it's just their
defense mechanism to protect their true
persona from coming out.
Which is their biggest fear, it shows them a
loss of power and control over you.
It's right there and then where they begin to
notice that you can really see right through
their mask.

"Healthy Love Ties"

Be with somebody who always fights for
you, not constantly fights with you.

"Irony at its Finest"

The thing is, you hold onto to hope for a person who doesn't hope to hold onto you.

"The Power"

Never give your fears the power to believe

they're real.

"The Betrayal"

I still feel heart broken after your return.

Nothing feels the same anymore.

Your kiss.

Your touch.

Your body.

They all feel different to me.

As if it belongs to someone else.

I try to find the person I fell in love with but

he just isn't there.

I have no clue who you are now and that's

the broken truth.

I'm lost trying to remember how all of this

went down.

In the blink of an eye, I wasted so much of

my time being stuck in the cycle of your

love lies.

"In Your Eyes"

Always remember...

The right person isn't meant to be perfect.

It's the person who in your eyes seems

perfect.

Someone who always reminds you of

yourself.

"Prove Them Wrong"

The craziest part is that they treat you the
way they do because you've always
allowed it and still haven't left.
In their mind they believe you'll truly never
leave, that's until you prove them wrong.

"Traumatized"

I invested so much of myself in you that I'm
afraid to invest in anyone else.
So, I only invest in myself.

"How Scars Are Made"

All the things we deeply love...

Will always be...

All the things we'll never forget.

"Pull Back"

At times in my life I feel like I ask for too
much.
Relationship wisc.
But that's not the case.
I'm just not being satisfied.
I'm not being understood.
I'm not being appreciated and that causes
me to pull back.

"I Wish You the Best"

I just hope that in the midst of it all, you're

happy with your decisions.

"Keep Your Head Up"

The most beautiful things will always be
right in front of you.

"Never Amount"

I won't try to replace you or do the

impossible task of forgetting you.

I'll just live with the memories of who you

could never amount to be.

"The Cycle"

It gets to the point where almost everybody
in your life slowly becomes like everybody
from your past.

"Turbulences"

Every emotion you feel today is meant to
be felt.
Whether it's good or bad.
Know that you are meant to experience
these random turbulences.
They are there for a reason.
They may drastically pull you up or down
but allow yourself to understand why they
are there in the first place.
This is how you connect and begin to
release everything that is no longer meant
to live within you.

"Infinite Light"

It's no secret.
The way you carry yourself is shown
through everything you do.
The way you can unapologetically be
yourself will always be the most fascinating
thing in you.
Your heart can break thousands and
thousands of times and still, you stand as if
nothing has gotten the best of you.
Your resilience and bravery is unmatched.
Your soul is indeed, one of a kind.
In a world full of sadness, you bring the sun
out.
Bringing everything that was once dead
back to life.
Believe that you are all these things and
more.
For you are divine.

You're the most beautiful, purest, brightest,

infinite light that our dear Lord has created.

"The Beginning and the End"

Healing isn't meant to be this smooth sailing journey.
It's actually quite like being in a storm but the difference is, that during this chaotic outcome you have this deep sense of knowing that eventually peace will come.
The harsh rain will stop and the clouds will slowly part ways, allowing the sun to shine through and it's in this moment you'll realize that all of these things are simply a part of life.
You can not control the things that happen around you, but you can control what occurs inside of you.
Meaning, the storm doesn't have to be a part of you.
It's just something that you need to witness and experience.

This combination allows you to see everything at a different perspective and this helps you to spiritually grow in life.
So, it's okay to break hundreds of times but what counts is how many times you can heal yourself.
Just always remember that it's not about the time frame or how far others are in their journey.
It's about you and learning how you can make it out of any situation.
You must adapt and have the ability to allow yourself to transform even in uncomfortable situations.
It's all a process to get closer to your highest self but it starts with making healthy choices and liberating yourself from anything and anyone that keeps you in a low vibration.

To vibrate high, you must first heal from

your own toxicity and the one's people

engraved in you.

It is not an easy task but with patience,

consistency, and determination it can be

done.

This is why the storm must happen

unexpectedly.

You're meant to change so don't be afraid

of the unknown.

It's only there to teach, redirect, and guide

you towards the path God originally

destined for you.

So, it's okay.

Feel the wrath of the storm but just keep

your faith in the one who knows the

beginning and the end.

"The Moment"

It will all make sense the moment you
decide you want it to.

"Superficial World"

It intrigues me how we all have the freewill
to perceive the world the way we want it to.
It is almost as if a test for you to define
what is and isn't important.
In a man made world filled of superficiality
you're given the choice to choose what truly
fulfills your soul.
Through this decision making you have
your intuition and the power of
discernment.
You also have the gift to see but you have
to question if what you're seeing is real.
This is what begins to separate the flesh
from the spirit and that is if you even decide
to make the separation to see the truth of
what lies beneath your thoughts and
feelings.

We chase after things that doesn't give us what we really desire and that's where you have to take a real look at what you're doing and ask yourself, "why?"
The answer will unfold itself the second you decide that you're ready to accept the truth because sometimes the problem isn't others, the problem is you and your freewill.
The choices you make today play a huge role in your future.
That's where you need to rethink and take control of what deserves to come with you tomorrow and for the rest of the days our beloved God blesses us with.
Today is literally the day you can decide to drop the baggage of all the things you no longer want to carry.
Anything negative shouldn't be allowed into your journey and that's the point.

Life wasn't created to be so complicating, it
only seems this way to you right now
because of all the people and things you've
welcomed into your life when you knew you
shouldn't have.
But the greatest gift of all of this is that you
have the ability to change and transform
things.
Your heart, mind, and soul has the power to
manifest anything that you want as long as
it's coming from a place of love and light.
Trust me, this superficial world has nothing
compared to what God has planned for
your life.

"Guard Your Heart"

There will be days where some things won't
make any sense and that's where things
begin to get intense.
But...
It's that same intensity that reminds you
how much of a human you really are.
So, many feelings just rushing throughout
your body.
Feelings...
No one can comprehend.
Because...
They belong to you and no one else.
Something...
No one will ever truly understand.
Something...
Only you can protect.

"Changes"

It's all in the memories.

They're the ones that change us.

Only because...

They're meant to.

"The Renewal"

An abrupt change in your life is the
beginning of something new.
It is God's way of renewing your spirit and
preparing you for what's to come.

"The Missing Piece"

You probably don't hear this as often as you
should but you're already, "whole."
The truth is, the world around you tries to
convince you that you need someone to
complete you but that's false.
All you need is to fulfill yourself first, then
destiny decides when someone deserves
to align with your stars.
You need to be content with who you are.
Meaning you need to learn how to be
happy in the same space that once made
you sad.
To do so, you must make peace with your
past and present.
You must accept all of your flaws and
imperfections.

Accept the mistakes you've made and let

go of all of your regrets because there's

nothing you can do about these things.

But...

Most importantly, love yourself

wholeheartedly through this awakening and

you'll see that you've been the missing

piece all along.

"Love Will Find You"

I bet you've been through the worst when it comes to relationships.
You've walked the face of this Earth believing that people carried the same heart as you, only to find out in the end that they left you traumatized towards something that's supposed to feel everlasting.
I honestly wish things were different for you and someone could've saved you from the heartbreaks.
But...
Destiny seems to have other plans.
I also wish I could tell you the real reason behind all of this, but I am made of all the little things that you're made up of.
I don't know it all, but I'll tell you this...

"To understand the true meaning of love,

you have to understand the meaning of

pain."

This is how life guides you towards all the

beautiful things that fulfills your soul.

For it is through the seeds of your tears

where your spirit grows.

In your toughest moments, you will break

but at the very same time, you will awaken.

Everyday is a new day for us to decide our

future.

It starts right here in this moment.

Literally, any moment and any day can

change the outcome of everything you fear

of today.

It could be for better or for worse.

The power is all in your hands.

What you let go and hold on to is all up to

you.

But it's important to say...

"Don't put too much weight on your heart."

Try your best not to carry memories of the past.

Those days of those horrible times have already passed.

Know that it will never happen again because you've spiritually grown.

It's just a matter of time.

But, trust me.

Love will find you.

If you would like to follow me on social media:

Instagram: Lanenapr22